The Biscuit Tins of England

Poems

Liz Atkin

IRON PRESS

First published 2003 by IRON Press
5 Marden Terrace
Cullercoats
North Shields
Northumberland
NE30 4PD
Tel/Fax:(0191) 253 1901
E-mail: seaboy@freenetname.co.uk

ISBN 0 906228 90 5

Printed by
Tyneside Free Press Ltd

FIRST EDITION

Typeset in Comic Sans 12pt
© poems, Liz Atkin
Cover painting: Larkstone Hill
by Peter Atkin

Book design by Faye Oliver
@IRONEye

IRON press is represented by
Inpress Ltd
1st Floor
52 Harpur St
Bedford
MK40 2QT
Tel: +44 (0) 1234 330023
Fax: +44 (0) 1234 330024
E-mail: jon@inpressbooks.co.uk
Web: www.inpressbooks.co.uk

LIZ ATKIN was born in Stamford, Lincolnshire in 1951. She trained as a visual artists at St. Martin's School of Art, London. She worked diligently for twenty years on large pencil drawings, exhibiting in Europe and the UK, culminating in a series of six feet square drawings of the Nativity performed by chimpanzees, exhibited in Edinburgh.

After flirting on and off with the notion of writing poetry she began to write seriously in 1994. Her first collection was published by Diamond Twig in 1999. Her work is widely published in poetry magazines and two anthologies. She is currently finishing her third collection.

She has lived in Newcastle upon Tyne since 1986.

Acknowledgements and thanks are due to the editors of the following magazines in which some of these poems first appeared.

Smiths Knoll, The Rialto, Aabye and Aabye's Baby, Other Poetry, Magma, Poetry Monthly, Konfluence, The Journal, The New Writer, Iota, Prop, Urthona, Pulsar, New Welsh Review, Seam, The Affectionate Punch, Skald.

'*Cow Wash*' first appeared in '*Glee with a Blue Background*'.

—— for Kath Lawson ——
with love and thanks

Contents

The Coach Party

entered the chill wondrous beauty
of the only Temple on their tour,
assorted footwear and cameras left
outside and simple slippers worn,
yet all they could see
were the shuffling feet
of one of their number
that no slippers could accommodate.

They'd never seen anything like it,
hideously distorted, bunion raddled,
big hammer toes twisted to lie along
a crossed and ingrown phalanx
all bearing the nicks and gouges
of chiropody, they talked about it
in subdued reverential whispers
for days after the visit.

The Secret

Whilst your father was hospitalised
we crept into his bedroom
to discover the secrets
of his Mason's attache case,

stale widower's curtains were drawn
and inside the spiderleg
and dottle darkness
of the bedside cupboard
an alarming splash
of pink potty startled us.

A single slab bed
and looming wardrobe
full of male shadow
that rattled with unclothed wires
as we pulled out the case

to find inside
packets of his favourite sweets
and breakfast cereal,
a pair of binoculars
and a heavy duty torch,

and lying on the bottom
a hand written timetable

of spaceships to Mars,

I watched your face confirm
the neighbours sightings
of an old man,
very like your father
in gaping night attire
seen waving a torch
at the night sky
on the Town Moor hill.

Tiger

In the laden silence before the storm
cars assemble at the lighthouse point
and park to face a sea
still and septic
beneath inflamed purple clouds,
windows are open
to thick warm air
as the lighthouse grows paler
against a rapidly darkening sky.

Suddenly a man shape tiger
in a sand clumsy stagger
appears on the empty beach,
driven by the stifling heat
to run amok from the High Street
and a charity collection tin.

A distant growl of thunder
rolls over the horizon
as the tiger prances in frustration
wrenching and pulling
to finally dislocate
gaping wide jaws
revealing a bolus of head
the apoplectic colour
of raw meat lodged inside.

As heavy drops fall
the tiger is on all fours
up the grassed slope
toward the cars,
and it is just possible
to hear the heavy tut of door locks
and see anxious smudges behind
overworked wipers trying
in vain to part the curtains.

Black Milk

At the heart
of the allotment shanty town
amongst higgledy sheds
and lurching fences
stands a large windowless hut
within a compound,
opening hours painted crudely
on a padlocked gate.

I have been inside,
gone past the slow man
sweeping a puddle
like brown mercury
around the yard
to the ex-miners
who run the place
in a fertile dark
that allows glimpses
of coal black labrador
shifting shadows with his tail.

In a smell of chicken manure,
Jeyes Fluid, garotta and lime,
by seed packets feeble
as weak bulbs in the dark
I've seen men come

dangling milk bottles
to be filled
from the fat bellied tank
shrouded in sacking
on two trestles
at the back of the hut.

A black viscous fluid
trickles from a tiny tap
in its umbilicus
belching and gurgling
as the men pat its sides,
these same men who sit
on their plots at night
hunched in skip salvaged chairs
attentive as midwives
watching over their vegetable monsters.

As if Hoping for a Cure

I saw them
on a trip out
to the Waterworks Open Day,
blue lipped and ankle ballooned,
pulses telling the wrong time
as they gasped by the settling tanks
while scale traction models
chugged enthusiastically over the grass.

They inched up the staircase
into the Victorian building
to stand small before
the breath taking
massive beam engine
nodding and rising
nodding and rising
steady and silent
pumping tall as a steeple
on kettles of oil and steam.

I see they've spurned the Tea Room
with its chocolate bakelite handles,
not wanting to sit folded
over murmuring muscles
listening to the tentative
knocking of faulty valves,

instead they stand meekly
outside the Pumping Room
hands pressed to the brickwork
as if hoping for a cure.

Asylum Laundry

A sedated inmate has just been separated
from his soul, a man size gingerbread
hacked from a bedsheet
that he carried everywhere
like a comforter, a chew chew or blanky,
sucking and canoodling,
sometimes eating it then yanking it back
panicky, hand over hand.

Grass stained, food smirched,
lipstick kissed on a hem,
stiff with secretions
he never let go of his filthy frayed soul,
but staff found the stench insufferable
and sent the sheet to the Laundry,
gothic outbuildings with a stationary clock
and hissing steam from knee level pipes,
where workers were accustomed
to little oddities such as
feather lined body linen
and knotted arms and legs.

Not deemed a delicate
through the wash house it went,
unsorted because bright colours excite,
receiving special attention from the Stain Girl

then on to the giant Hydro-Extractor
followed by the starching machine,
next a drying cabinet,
a wardrobe the size of a caravan
full of warm summer breezes,
before the Finishing Room
where it was hand ironed
and folded to the size of a handkerchief
stopping just short of a neatly sewn monogram.

His Laugh

A childs body was found
clothing torn open and discarded
in a dingy hotel room,
the sort we've all seen
in movies, flickering
with neon through the night.
A room that would be
familiar to Weegee or Arbus,
full of evidence
in the tortured bed,
décor snow scattered
amongst the blood
and long white hairs
tweezered from a soap sliver
in the sooty handbasin.
Specimens of reindeer faeces
were lifted from worn carpet
and sent for analysis
and since the night it happened
the neon sign
which had simply stated 'Hotel'
has only lit and flashed
the first two letters
sending hollow laughter
into the winters night.

The Tomb

I try to imagine her body
understone pale with whalebone
bunkered away below the pavement
on the seafront promenade,
twelve steps down and round
onto sandy mosaic tiles.

Her attendants door never replied
and she was rarely seen
due to dense net and kettle steam
blurring a gas fire smudge
and budgie blotch of colour.

It must be so silent now,
no thump and slam of cubicle doors
fastened with brass bolt slide,
the rustle and sigh,
the dribbling streams that became
a roaring flush - just the sound
of the sea lapping up the bowls
and beetles cavorting in the tip saucer.

At night a urine yellow light
still seeps up through
the thick glass blocks
cordoned off by wrought ironwork,

and I think she's down there,
sealed in by slapdash breeze blocks
that are fronted with
a rusting grille primly
clutching its padlock handbag.

The Woman from Rectory Road

if only they were
the old still-born kind
leaving no illusion
with their rigid finger splay
clicking lids and painted hair,
the rigor mortis limbs
that had to be wrenched
to dress and undress
in home made knits.
Upended to utter
they would often end up
battered and scribbled upon,
silent little heroines
tied to the radiator grille
of the municipal dustcart.

Now these new ones
are infants with heartbeats
and new born wristbands
plus six life-like functions,
they babble and burp
cuddle and dribble
soil and sleep
for marginally less
than the cost of a second hand cot,

and they also lure
the woman from Rectory Road
who surreptitiously loiters
in the noisy department
with her face made up
for 'just looking thank you'
and her snatching chastised
fingers gloved yet yearning.

Wet Concrete 1949

If I were a paleontologist
with my nose to the pavement
in years to come
would I wonder at these,
not the normal pedestrian plod
but impressions of petrified poise,

set in the concrete they suggest
a four legged living thing
with hard and soft side
that moved with two heart tempo

and would I flesh out
these fossil prints
and turn time back in the
anti-clockwise of ballrooms
to see the couple's
one giddy moment
as they waltzed their way home?

An Elegant Hearse

Brisk daughters emptied out
your cluttered flat
into the yellow skip,
staple tins, beans and peaches,
born in rationing days,
a hoarder's hundred of
locks and hinges prised
from discarded doors,
frayed plugs, toothbrushes,
and decades of newspaper
topped off with flowers
that died with your sudden illness.

Whilst they were attending
the crenellated crematorium
sitting smokeless on false lawns
I watched you swing up into the air
held secure under netting
and your walking stick forgotten
hanging from the skip lip
tapping jauntily as in life.

Genealogy

I walk through the caravan park
on a chilly December morning
drawn by the name, Sandy Bay.

They're all closed up of course
either curtained or emptied
with notes as polite as milk
requests for the robbers saying
there is nothing of value within,

some have rustic trellises
and benches of beach driftwood,
all have calor gas cylinders
standing sentinel at the door.

The Amusements are mute and shrouded
the chippy closed and odourless,
and those with the best sea view
teeter on the edge of erosion now.

I walk for hours up and down
the alphabetical rows, see how
some are leaking to death
but I'm looking for that pile

of sand at the doorstep,

the sea stained sandals kicked off,
the rubber bucket full of starfish
next to bread and potato pebbles,

and I keep on walking in the silence
amongst cream and white boxes
in close rows as far as the eye can see,
coffins of past summer holidays
and not one of them distantly mine.

Tongues

Lambs tongues are taken, severed
from their cleft bleat holes
and washed to remove extraneous
mucous, matter and slime,
then packed in mute dozens
soaked in brine and cured,
blanched and canned,
to represent a delicacy for some.

And as these gourmands eat,
as their own wagging muscle
in its saliva pool tastes then bites
into a dumb relative, moving
it around that eagar orifice
before pushing it back down
then licks the lips and welcomes more,
lets urge them on to overeat,
to finish the lot and winewash it down
then slip into a comatose state,

so that their tongue, a large
fat and furred malodorous organ
can fall back too, curling up
on itself to block the airway,
putting a lid on a final meal.

An Escaped Prank

The student's alligator
inspired terror, the thought
of it hiding in the ooze
of the dehydrated boating lake,
that broken grin of sixty eight
interlocking teeth hidden by
wrecks and sodden bread.

Nowhere was safe, the exposed
carpet of bowling green waiting
for the trenched drag of tail,
the closed café with hastily
stacked flimsy white furniture,

eggs could be lying in the soil
hatching in the heat wave,
legs and dogs stayed away
from every rustle in the undergrowth

that became a rumbling stomach
clinking with the indigestible
bracelet and butterfly hair slide
of the missing six year old.

Birds were silent
and the floral clock stopped,

logs in the duck pond were shot
by council workmen making old women
jump on their 'in memoriam' benches,

and in the Sunday morning quiet
of faint chimes and distant dog bark,
a jogging youth in the park
suddenly runs full pelt and frantic.

Funeral Retrospective

The models arrive
in chronological order
to process in single file
down the narrow aisle,
each one stark naked

but for heels and hats
and one Venus in Gloves,
beauties gone beyond blowsy
carrying their drapes
of fur and velvet to the empty pews

where they arrange themselves
posing as they did for him
after gin and cream cakes
from his rusting fridge.

Reclining, seated, sprawled,
full-frontal standing,
decaying femme fatales
blue veins knotting
as they root for the earth,
their facial pigment paste
slapped over a greenish base,

each one holds her pose

in the church chill
motionless but for spasms
and the tiniest dribble
over creeping goose flesh
for a full forty five minutes

whilst the artist's wife,
eyes clotted with cataracts
sits alone in her wheelchair,
dressed and rug wrapped
and firmly tucked in.

Embroidery

They're sold on Blackpool pier,
cheap, machined lace hangings
eighteen inches square
that depict in empty white
a rural cottage in tea cosy thatch
by tumbling brook
with snow capped mountains behind
and in the sky hang the words
'No place like Home'.

Who would live in such a place?
maybe a gillie or a gamekeeper
years ago, but now it would be
the holiday home of the very rich
employing a man in the garden
judging by the abundance
of lupins, foxgloves,
and roses round the door,

and contrary to the handwritten sign
in the shop that says
'no embroidery required'
I think that the people shuffling
along this piss smelling pier
with its scattered chips and vomit
and gypsies lurking behind nets

with their beckoning fingers of fate,
would have an enormous amount
of embroidery to do to make
this image resemble what they know as home.

Dead Marys

I know of Hail Marys, Contrary Marys,
Bloody Marys, Virgin Marys,
and the four scottish queens,
but the dead Marys I choose to remember
lived in my old council block.

Fat Mary found everything comical
and when she wasn't eating large
lap suppers from the Cornucopia chippy
her mouth watered for cakes
so sweet they sweated.
Partial to the pop in her heyday
she'd piss giggling in the gutter
but then her days got cumbersome
wedged in an armchair
on top of a towel in case. She died
in her weekly bath jammed tight
into the cold enamel coffin,
her cast off nightie sudsy on the floor.

Deaf Mary lived opposite on nicotine
and lipstick, entertaining male visitors
until her bones poked through,
she fell from her bed in winter,
snapping and splintering, and lay there
for days unable to make herself heard.

Little Mary was a child size pensioner
rattling round on the ground floor,
she'd recite her ailments alphabetically
punctuated with pills.
Every day she'd be peeping over
her front room windowsill waiting
for the missing third letter to grow
in her gullet and starve her to death.

Case History

Miss P. presented
with total loss of voice,
a spinster of 54 living with
and looking after her elderly mother,
she indicated a constriction in her chest,
mimed her voice being strangled,
and whispered that she woke many times
at night choking and gagging.
Over a period of time
the precipitating factor slowly emerged
that every evening for over a year
Miss P. had been a wireless,
having accidentally broken the original
and treasured set, she was made to sit
on the hard kitchen chair
with a cardboard box over her head
in which her mother had shaped
a mouth hole covered with mesh.
She had to tell moral tales,
sing hymns and forecast the weather
ending with a prayer at 9.30 p.m. promptly,
but now of course all her mother heard
was the static sound of susurrus
which so enraged her that she rapped
her wireless repeatedly with marble

hard knuckles and shouted
in her bomb blast voice.

Hitman

A masked
lone gunman
was spotted running away
from the scene
in the autumn dusk,
running away from the body
shot twice in the head,
neighbours are watching T.V.
and only hear backfires
as he runs over wasteground
on the council estate
a sawn-off in his waistband,

and keeps on running
there is no getaway car,
but see how his hand
now slaps his hip
urging his horse on
and how the other grips
reins tight in front
as they gallop and leap
breath whinnying,
then come to open fields
and he slows to a trot,
dismounts and pats
the sweating flanks

before leaving the horse
tied to a fence post
secure in the knowledge
that it will never be found.

Cow Wash

The bare bones remain,
a rusting framework
in the field behind
the now derelict byre,
clothed in village rumour

that tells how it was built
inside a canvas tunnel
with a conveyer nudging
the short horn herd along
in single file toward
a chamois and suds
warm water wash
of udders and quarters first,
then rotating body brushes
electrically driven
alternating firm and soft
followed by a straw wisp tickle
for massage and circulation
before being buffed by
waves of sultry air.

They say the local men
became incensed at hearing
the cows shrieking and giggling
way after milking and on

late into the night
and so
burnt the contraption down.

Snake

I overheard the adult whispers
about the dead seamstress
further down our street
and the poisonous snake,

twelve feet long
and painstakingly stitched
by her thimbled fingers
in discarded black-out fabric,
it slithered from the gas supply
to her bedsit death bed
where drawstring jaws were clamped,
pulled tight and knotted over her face.

Every night for months I dreamt
her skin a scary cherry red
inside her best fox fur,
the hissing snake on top
of its willing prey,
black mouth full of gassy kisses.

I can't remember her name
but I do know now, years later,
the sibilant name of the snake.

The Parlour

Just the ground floor
in any anonymous terrace,
front window double netted
and the no-number door
admitting only a certain ring
into a polished waiting room
with samplers on sepia walls
and high seated chairs auctioned
from past institutional life.
The corner holds a tea urn
and a gossiping budgie
perched above eggs for sale
stacked in grey trays between
back numbers of Stitchcraft.

In the next room Miss Smith
works under daylight bulbs
making the tiniest of stitches
using fine surgical needles
and bright fast silks
to embroider her ladies skin,

roses and violets are bread and butter
along with daisy chain necklaces,
butterflies and overweight cherubs
in under smalls places

or concealing operation scars,

she will not do anchors, snakes,
or skull and cross bones
and instead of tigers she prefers
a dear deceased pussy cat.

You'll never see her photograph
like those men with dirty fingernails
in a cloud of fag smoke
bent over a bulging bicep,
she moves from city to city
like a peripatetic chiropodist
and as for her best work….
The Last Supper in thirty colours
is currently in a Hospice
soon to be buried or burnt.

Dropped Stitches

The Wool Box has closed
leaving naked mannequins
and old women
whose fingers pointed
and looped in the language
of Wendy and Patons
cast off from a time
when everything was knitted.

Egg warmers for the girls,
socks and bathers for the boys,
chunky pullovers for him,
cosy bedjackets for her,
all to the constant natter
of deft and fluent fingers
sharpening the pins
that once savagely pierced
the unwanted unborn.

The Church Hall will raffle
the twenty two babies
found at the back of the shop,
knitted in pure white
and stuffed to an exact
nine pounds in weight,
clothed in bootees and bonnets

and stitch perfect matinée coats,
each one is embroidered
on the forehead with
a birthmark rash of surname.

A Sense of Foreboding

settled on me
as I watched a woman brushing
her small daughter's head
of golden hair on the Metro platform.

Long, bright, resplendently blonde,
the child turned slowly
under the emphatic strokes
basking beneath her spotlight,
a slight smile peeping through
the veil of crowning glory.
I didn't like the way her fingers,
slightly stiff, splayed away
from her pretty summer frock.

Half a dozen men from the offices
in their dark suits
watched attentively,
women bound townwards stared
with tired eyes, one or two
reaching up to touch lustreless heads.

The old woman next to me
wrapped in her wheelchair
pointed a knotted, wavering finger,
her crackling voice dribbling gibberish

to a carer behind
as the train pulled in
and the child bounded on
running ahead of her mother,
the sort of child who would
refuse to hold hands.

I didn't get on, staying behind
to pick up the golden tangle
tugged from the brush and dropped,
before any of the others did.

Last Seen

I saw a pair of Hook-a-Ducks
in plump plastic, features outlined
in grime, with simple rusty
question marks screwed into their skulls
bobbing down the wide Tyne,

leaving a lifetime of going clockwise
every afternoon and evening
in the fairground hubbub
jostling with siblings
beneath string loops swooping
for an easy prize every time.

Who had lured them
ever buoyant but buffeted
by boat wakes and tide,
to hear the distant anxious cry
of the car alarm bird
and feel the cold, unseen nudgings
in the black below, no longer
painted blue and two inches deep.

Now youths strain from jetties
well out of reach, so throw
stones and half bricks,
and as they reach the open sea

past fishermen gathered
round the piss bottomed lighthouse
who try with telescopic rods

I imagine their smile of beak curve
is still firmly fixed as they wonder
where the quiet secluded duckpond
they were promised is.

'We Can Alter Anything'

Such a small shop
for so large a claim,
just a glass fronted cupboard
in the market arcade
with a counter leaving space
for no more than two customers
rubbing shoulders with
a racked queue of clothes.

A 'qualified staff'
of two ancient women
sit waiting at machines,
pin prick eyes behind thick lenses
know in an instant squint
all about taking in and letting out,
turning up or not,
shortening or lengthening
the lined and underlined.

The big bellied teapot
that sits between them
constantly warm, tells of women's
labour, never mind the light relief
of the panto-cow that came in
last Christmas gone, and I watch

53

women shuffling through the market
down trodden, threadbare and care worn,
raw fingers lugging heavy
intestinal pink carrier bags,
but none of them,
not one single disenchanted one of them
enters this small shop
with its huge reckless promise.

Sweet little old ladies

a weekly pilgrimage
to the ground floor
opposite cold cuts and cakes
sees them queuing before
the brightly coloured glass wall.

A young woman in white coat
and nurse-neat hat dispenses
requests with a prescription rattle
into the giant scale pan,
wrapped or silent, glaces,
gems, pastilles or drops,
old favourites bagged
in the plump paper of childhood.

When one collapses
as they often do,
brittle and malnourished
on parma violets and soup,
bones are patted and wigs
re-aligned as they're helped
to the chair by the lifts.

Hankies are worried
from thin sleeves as the sweet
that fell from the mouth

is swiftly found, glistening
like a glass eye to be popped back
between blue lips as if
it were a sugar coated soul.

Showhome

She went on a Tuesday afternoon
to the new estate, built on the
once glorious cowslip meadows
and entered the pristine sanctity
of one of many family showhomes
each with a pretentious name,
she put on the blue plastic overshoes
like elongated shower caps, provided
to prevent her dirt walking in.

A single, middle aged nullipara
who had never gone upstairs to bed
in a life of rented rooms and flats
now shuffles around bedrooms one to four
all double glazed and white painted wood,
looks down upon the garden turf square
with standard cherry tree, whose
fallen blossom the new occupants
will be sure to call pink snow,

then, thumbs hooking down under
skirt she squats in the middle
of fitted oatmeal carpet and evacuates
her bowels of three substantial meals
in a warm stinking pile, tapered off
with a triumphant trumpeting note.

A Few Minutes in a Western

I left the country lane to climb
the sudden, towering slag mountain,
blue grey baked and cinderous
a steep and narrow path wound up
to a vast plateau, a prairie cracked
with fissures, stamped with hoof prints.

The midday sun was scorching down,
the expected pool not there,
just crumbling canyons full
of bottomless shadow and bone white wood,
the remains of an old trading post.

Now I noticed the dead trees,
strange spiky weeds and buffalo skulls
near shrugged snake skins, above me
wheeling birds cried mournfully
then shrieked, at first concealing
the distant curdling whoops and yells

of Apaches on the warpath.
I crouched and ran, scrambling
and slipping back down the path
arriving anxious at the bottom,
then turned and looked up to see
a line of boys watching me,

each one straddling a bike and motionless
in a fringe along the skyline.

Application for a Hermit's Dwelling

I wouldn't want that vacant cave,
that rock scooped riverside hovel
with its fingernail hewn shrine –
I lack the religious conviction.

I think I'm more suited to the island
in the middle of the boating lake
hidden but for the occasional
alarming glimpse of bird limed face
and living on thrown and sodden bread,

or the topmost highrise flat
with its sealed up letter box
and all wires cut, just pigeons
on the balcony from where I'd fly
my cabbage white kite covered in urgent scribble.

Maybe a derelict allotment shed or
the roundabout island in a sea
of constant traffic, its verges strewn
with hubcaps and litter, and I could
sit amongst the dead municipal blooms and ......

but now you tell me that since visions
are no longer a requirement of tenure
the waiting list has lengthened,

and you point out of your office window
to the top ledge of the N.C.P. opposite
where hundreds crouch in their carapace
of fixed scowl like so many gargoyles,
each one an arms length apart.

One day

The sky above the pigeon lofts
is stippled daily
with spasmodic formation flying
by pampered birds with map pin eyes.

I prefer their city centre cousins
crowding the parks for pastie crumbs,
underfoot C.C.T.V. extras who,
by night are accidentally shut
in the shopping mall,
an airy aviary
with stationary escalators,
switched off fountains
and an audience of rigid mannequins
behind their deceptive glass

as they soar and swoop
from level to empty level
showing us how it will be one day.

It's that time of year

when post boxes have their mouths stuffed,
when streets are choked with fallen forest
as men shoulder dying conifers
to a glittering gaudy death.

Thin suspicious Santas lurk
barely disguised, inside garden sheds
snowballed with décor snow
in Supermarket foyers.

The city gypsies switch
from hawking lavender to mistletoe
waving it beneath faces stiff
as the nativity automata in the mall,

though there is a flicker of something,
some electrical surge clicking
in the impassive shepherd's face
as his crook thrashes down unnoticed
into the laden manger.

It's that time of year when last buses
pull into depot cathedrals
with oil black floors and single neon strips
flickering with the ghosts of a thousand moths,

terminated buses full of fetid breath
and steamed up windows
with head size holes rubbed
where empty faces once hung.

Almost Extinct

The rest of him is stained and crumpled
but this, as if a precious thing,
is kept immaculately folded,

palsied hands fumble it out and lift
the edges
the way he'd look inside a sandwich,
then re-align, pat, and put away,

preserving shape from when she would
borax boil the whole flock
to remove secretions and whiten,
then smooth and fold, smooth and fold.

Once he'd let it flutter
at station farewells and before
it lost dexterity and cunning –
lay eggs to entertain,

but now it lies alone each night
with its faded monogram

the last one
in the wardrobe he built years ago
from a dismantled pigeon loft.

The Future Left Behind

Spanish City Funfair in winter
locked up and shuttered down,
the only cries those of gulls
perched on the twisted white
spine of the roller coaster,
the haunted house boarded up
screams muted to X-Ray murmurs.

The Gypsy's done a bunk
leaving a fortune telling hut
no bigger than a garden shed,
windows stripped of mis-spelt
signs and celebrity cuttings,
just petticoat tears of nets left

which afford a peep at
thin partition separating
a damp carpet waiting room
from the inner sanctum
of two chairs and formica table

on which, surprisingly left behind
like a dead T.V. set
glass eye blind, is her crystal ball
cupped in two pale plaster hands.

This makes such a mockery
of the long silent queue
that waited all summer
in battered slippers,
careworn women
some with bandaged hands
clutching a fiver's worth of fate.

Look

they line up with their binoculars
and cameras
to peep through the purpose built
holes in the wall
at birds on the sanctuary lake,
whilst a field away
behind their backs,
a pink elephant stands with a log
in its tusks
and an empty howdah on its back,
going slowly white in the North East
chill
on the fringes of the caravan park.

Arkcraft

I've seen the colour before
in day old jam jars of paint water
back in primary school.

Now it is everywhere
drowning all landlocked familiarity
leaving just skymark tips
of vane and aerial,

there are worms,
distended and pale
in wriggling knots amongst
sodden litter and house contents.

Rain withdrew after twenty days
leaving an unpocked boating lake
as far as the eye could see
beneath a sky the colour
of an old cistern,

a pensioner with budgie
rocks by in a pram,
families in patched dinghies
cuddling quilt wrapped T.V.s,
an inflatable paddling pool
empty but for a puddled message

of flood coloured vomit
containing alphabet soup,

they all eddy and whirl
inexpert ballroom dancers
bumping into bloated cattle corpses
above the submerged bunting of washing lines.

On the high ground
a joblot of retired lifeboats
filled to the gunnels with soil
and planted out with municipal floral crew.

Fifi

No chump chimp me
despite my poodle name,
fifty years in captivity
that given my Keeper's key
I could unlock anytime I chose.

When younger I was up
to all the mimicking antics,
self applauding hair brushing
and use of a knife and fork,
lapping up the fearsome grins
when I rode a bike and roller skated,
then after hours playing cards
and smoking with the Keepers.

My first born daughter
became a T.V. star
not my cup of tea,
ten years later they took
my son to be an astronaut,
now his body orbits earth
in its canister, round and round
in a celestial version
of cage pacing here –
and I was left, the matriarch
at the daily Tea Party

each afternoon at three,
pouring and passing,
pouring and passing.

Now every rotten yellow tooth
in my threadbare skull aches,
my bones are filled
beneath doormat fur
with the cold cracked concrete
of these retirement quarters
with their hanging tyre nooses
and I want to die
but as a chimpanzee -
not emulating humans to the end
and craving one last fag.

The Modern Day Lay Out for Young Enthusiasts

No need to worry about the trains,
there aren't any,
nothing to run as regular
as Hornby clockwork up in the attic
for hobby time hours on end.

These once scenic, now disused lines
lie unpicked and weed choked,
yet populated with various models,
see Boys A and B in the old siding
each with a half brick in hand,

and placed at intervals in realistic
undergrowth, 'to scale' carrier bags
from a choice of supermarket
containing an unidentified baby corpse.
The farm fields of your fathers day

are gone, in their place instant housing,
packs of 50 assembled in minutes,
and the glass pond from Mother's
handbag lies smashed with shopping trolleys.

The poles of semaphoring signals
have been axed, the signal box

used for sniffing and sex then burnt,
the station kit is ready derelict and vandalised

and comes with one waiting figure
to stand on the platform for years
a suitcase full of anxieties
moulded to his legs,
a blank, plastic face but for
the ticking side effects of medication.

Two Girls Dancing.

the sneaky X-Ray showed you dancing
belly to belly,
heads thrown back
two hands locked in triumphant tango
the other pair waist round,
heels kicking up gleefully
in a dizzying cavort.

So knives and blunted forceps
scooped you from dark cosiness
conjoined and interlocked
sharing a tummy of soft intestine,
they talk of splitting, cleaving,
and fifty-fifty chances for
Gemini girls tightly holding hands
as you're air-lifted but not dropped.

Two girls can't dance together
all their lives
sleeping lip on cheek
with legs entwined in hug,
fifteen men will do their utmost
to see you separated
throwing cold water
on your prancing dance,
a harsh arc of icy shock

just as their stiff wives
sever jammed fornicating dogs,
six legged monsters
that stray and stagger
into their spotless landscape.

The Biscuit Tins of England

are small airtight museums
for things that no longer need
to breathe, opened maybe twice
a year depending on location.

Absently packed by factory girls
each on her individual variety
Jam Sandwich Crème day after day
or Bourbons week by week,
filling the space, filling the tier
of Family Select Assortments

that become Christmas gifts
and lowly raffle prizes before
arrangement on 4 o'clock doilies.

Once the last favourite has gone
they come into their own
to house fossils and old photographs
not fit for the album, buttons,
letters and sewing bits. Some go to
garden sheds for seeds, screws
or sharp sand, others underbed
or wardrobe deep with secrets
and old nylons. A few are buried,
suburban time capsules containing

curled dead pets, exhibits and evidence
and one or two have even sailed,
the real ships biscuit with message,

and yet they long for the call,
not saucepans and railings this time,
but for the Biscuit Tins of England
to stack themselves high and solid
presenting rusting teatime faces.

Christmas time

It began with the toddler
screaming and crying
blue murder
as he was dragged up to the street level
from the metro station
into the drizzling December day.

In a matter of minutes
his mother was crying
her face crumpled and pouring,
then everyone in the street
was howling, sobbing and weeping.
In the shops and malls,
on buses, in taxis,
men were grunting and gasping
their faces distorted and wet,
some women stood, tears streaming,
features blurred, others blubbered
in doorways or leant against walls.
News vendors slumped on their stools
heads buried in damp newsprint,
pensioners snivelled and young men
fought wracked and shaking shoulders.

Everything ground to a halt in the city
beneath the pale disc of sun dissolving

in grey, carols tinkled somewhere
beneath the bawled outpouring of misery
and the toddler, that bloody toddler,
stood quietly, unafraid and smiling
by his shuddering mother.

Skye Leopard

They say you live in a cave
and shop in the Co-op
twice a year
wrapped up in an old tarpaulin,

that years ago you laid your body
before a Brighton tattoo artiste
clad in blood spattered vest and fag smoke,
and asked for the effect of sunlight
seen through African foliage
all over your skin,
not forgetting pads on palms and soles
and ears on top of a shaven head.

They say you escaped from Bertram Mills
to live on this wet island,
sightings are rare
of you preying and prowling
in faded buff,
though when dogs and lambs disappear
it is of course to slake
a blood thirst in your lair
say the island men
who dream of big game hunting.

Because you are so rarely seen

the stores will sell
a vivid coloured postcard
of a big cat leering
if they're not all sold out
to the local children
who lie stiff and silent
as Barbie dolls at night
listening to your purring breath
as, shy of the hen house,
you scrabble vegetables from the gardens
and they say nothing
understanding well,
the game of let's pretend.

The Real Bibles

are unearthed in elderly house clearance
to appear, stained and reeking
of sick room suffering
in second hand and charity shops,

Everybody's, Home and Family,
illustrated in century turn monochrome
with the occasional rash
of vivid colour warning.

They once held pride of place
handled only by the women,
and reverential whispered tones
were used for page after page

of alphabetical ailments
from Aleppo Buttons and Dhobie Itches,
bed bugs, blains and blistering blood,
knock knee knuckles, fidgets and tics,

to Grey Matter Spasm, Shopgirls Disease,
Summer Diarrhoea and Dirt Eating,
and then the hot, bitter, water brash
of heart burning Saints

and their hysterical dancing.

Trismus, truss and tongue tumours
speak of black mortification
and you can be sure

that the delicate green hue
of abdominal decay is illustrated.
Recipes for home made emollients
are offered, but not a single miracle,

just the white grin
of a pig bite scar on page 210
amongst the agony and the instructions
on individual wrapping of coals

for the deathly silent
sick room grate.

The Children Who Never Saw the Sea

went twice weekly
to the Light Department
from the wards,
dressing gowns clenched over
knitted bathers or underwear.

Subsized child bodies mishapen
with rickets and tubercular joints,
pigeon chests and wasting,
most are wheeled down
the olive green tiled corridors
braying coughs trotting ahead

into the dark room coloured
with the smell
of creosote and cinnamon oil
where the big lamp stands
full of mercury and argon gas
isolated in its painted circle.

The nurse hands out pairs
of black cartoon goggle eyes
and settles them on heavy chairs
(some doctors cast off furniture)
around the circle edge
for their tonic bathing

in three minutes of ultra-violet rays,

and there they sit with eyes closed
stiff, no fidgeting,
listening to the seagull spread
of wings behind the nurses head,
the unforgiving seats forbidding
any deckchair slump
as they try to build castles
in their heads
with egg timer sand
until the alarm clock rings
and the sun goes off.

The Dowser's Daughters

One lies drowning in her mind
bed bound by the weight
of a sodden head
that is swollen taut, skin tight
and hair scant over
a flooded skull vault.

The other is a double headed
two legged creature
in the nearby fields,
astride a trotting broom handle
up a sackcloth stuffed horses head
that she will dip and dunk to drink
repeatedly at hidden underground troughs.

In the darkened room
the grotesque head swells
squashing its small fretful face
so that she can not see
from protruding stagnant eyes.
Her diminished body begins to convulse

and somewhere in the next county
her father stands, gripping
his forked hazel twig,
his divining rod

that leaps and bucks violently
in his pale hands
like an unbroken horse.

Lament

First they ousted the kittiwakes
from their Baltic Mill roost,
then they netted all buildings
in a see-through Christo frenzy
to rid the city
of its so called flying rats

They're ankle deep in old chips now,
plus curry sauce, bright kebab stuffing
and pastie remnants, the street
sweepers can not cope and weekend
vomit clogs and chokes the gutters,

what's more stone dignitaries have shrunk
without them, and closed circuit TV
ratings have fallen, but most
importantly of all there's a rumour
that pigeon milk secretions mixed
with fine feathers and liquid shit
hold the ancient masonry together.

Now amongst the luckless citizens
of this crumbling city one or two
oddly dressed can be seen, standing
still as statues in the filthy park,
their outstretched palms stippled

with grain and faces pleading
with an empty leaden sky.

The Cuckoo House

She inherited the madness
from her clockmender father,
a terraced house turned
into a Tyrrolean chalet
with wooden deer on tiptoe
in the alpine rockery
and plywood, paint peeling, fir trees.

He had embellished with deep eaves
and ornate shutters decorated
in what looked like barge art,
and the final touch that drove
her mother out – a giant clock face
over the front window, its mechanism
filling the darkened parlour,
tangling up the stairwell
to the huge papery bellows in the box room.

The whole house ticked
to her father's heart beat
and left a shiver in her face
that is still there
as she does the weekly wind,
an old woman eating bible pages
and hearing on the hour, every hour,

the distorted bellows
worn down to a mournful one note
as the giant mechanical bird
bangs on the nailed up shutters
of her attic bedroom.

A Poem for the Bottle Banks

Black frock swirling
the priest sweeps
his inner city churchyard,

the broken glass all shades
of booze brown, clear and green,
carolling above the traffic roar,

from the smile on his face
you'd think he was sweeping
the fallen autumnal leaves

from stained glass trees.

Suitcase

'it eats no meat' your Father said
as he took the suitcase
for storage under the spare bed.
But how could he be so sure
that this battered, well travelled,
corners knocked off suitcase
was strictly vegetarian?
We've all heard of the trunk
left at Charing Cross station,
and numerous others in left luggage
and bus depot lockers,
carnivores all, engorged and stuffed
with flesh, limbs chopped up small,
organs separated and parboiled in one
as if to aid digestion.
I just hope that empty suitcase
keeps it's wide mouth firmly closed
and doesn't persuade your Mother
that she'd like to pack herself off
on a sudden, uncharacteristic holiday for one.

The Noddle

Her body stands in an ornate
one person bandstand of fussy
white Victorian marble,
forcibly drowned for her beliefs
the Virgin Martyr of the Waters
is minus her head, decapitated
in one clean slice
for pious pigeons to perch on.

Many wonder as to the whereabouts
of that missing head, does it lie
on a pillow in some citizen's bed,
kissed cold and chilly nightly,
or at the bottom of a garden pond
forgotten and reliving her death,
maybe taken by prankish revellers
in exchange for a traffic cone,
or perhaps inside a rotting suitcase
in left luggage at the station?

I'll tell you where her head is,
it stands on a small shelf
in the Market Square Ladies
right outside the Attendant's Room
with a backdrop of nicotined net.
She's been there for years

disguised in an auburn wig
with just a suggestion of lipstick,
her eyes are demurely lowered
to a saucer on the table below
where patrons give thanks for
soft paper and hot and cold running water.

The Da Vinci Prize

Men with butterflies in their stomachs
cocooned in home made contraptions
bred of hobby kits and airfix,
prepare to launch themselves
at a lumbering run off Bognor Pier
to plummet thirty feet straight down
in pantomimic idiocy
into the cold grey sea
to rapturous screams and applause.

The other contestants mostly come
from the land of the Indian rope trick
with it's intimate knowledge
of hiding places in the sky,
which makes it far worse
to know they fall with fatal
regularity at the exact same spot
in south west London,
dropping dead, frozen solid,
from a Boeing's wheel casing
into the plentiful land
of a superstore carpark.

Recent Books
from
IRON Press

Dead Poets' Cabaret
David Cobb

ISBN : 0 906228 88 3   *Price £7.00*

In David Cobb's extraordinary book, the author travels the British Isles to locate the tombstones of more than eighty acclaimed anglophone poets. A photo (and where applicable, epitaph) of each gravestone is complemented by pen pictures of the poets and Cobb's own cryptically comic clerihews .

Biting Back: *new fiction from the North*
Editor: Kitty Fitzgerald

ISBN: 0 906228 76 X   *Price: £6.99*

A new collection of mouthwatering stories from writers skilled at their craft commissioned to write for this landmark book, which affirms the upsurge of new fiction talent in the North of England. The dozen authors include: David Almond, Chaz Brenchley, Chrissie Glazebrook, Wendy Robertson.

Please add 75p per book p & p. Cheques to IRON Press
(address on page 2)
Check out our web site: www.ironpress.co.uk